CHURCHILL

THE MAN OF THE CENTURY

A Pictorial Biography

Purnell 1965

Edited by NEIL FERRIER

65-2491

PURNELL
1965

Only two months before his death Sir Winston Churchill made what was to be his last brief public appearance at the window of No. 28 Hyde Park Gate. The occasion was his 90th birthday in November 1964. On Friday 15th January 1965 the news was flashed around the world that the great statesman had had a stroke. The gravity of the news was felt by everybody. The world watched anxiously Sir Winston's last great battle. A silent, waiting crowd was never absent from the vicinity of his London home. Enquiries from all over the world were made hourly, relatives, friends and representatives of many nations visited him. Lord Moran (left), Sir Winston's physician and personal friend was constantly in attendance and his frequent bulletins kept the world informed of Sir Winston's progress. Lady Churchill was always by her husband's side.

The prayers of the humble, the tributes of the great, the solemnity of the funeral were all evidence of the depth of feeling, the affection, gratitude and honour in which the whole world held this noble descendant of Marlborough, this citizen of the world.

CHURCHILL—AN APPRECIATION

The death in his ninety-first year of Sir Winston Churchill removes from the contemporary scene a statesman whose services to his country are unexampled in modern times, one to whose courage, clear-sightedness and gift for leadership the world owes many debts of gratitude. Yet if we must remember him for one thing above all, it is bound to be for the inspiration, the will to fight on, that he injected into this country and her allies in the dark days of 1940.

He did not achieve this ability by accident. It was the logical culmination of a way of life and a way of thought.

To win wars the qualities required are courage, foresight, an absolute confidence in ultimate success, combined with an infinite patience, the power of judging in the heat of the fray both men and events, tireless energy and the ability to draw from others, over long periods, the best they can give, individually and in concert.

All these qualities Churchill possessed in an exceptional degree.

From his youth onwards he had seen war as the ultimate test of a man's reality. No firebrand—though often labelled one—he had gravitated to wars like a scholar to books, offering himself the heightened apprehension of existence their danger provided as a necessary part of the complete life. As a subordinate he could be wilful and scornful of those in authority, but nothing within his purview was ever allowed to stagnate and his loyalty once given was absolute.

Probably the most vital period of his apprenticeship as a leader was that which he spent with Lord Fisher at the Admiralty. Here was a man whose weaknesses in human relations had as much to teach him as his professional vision and sheer pertinacity. During those years of preparation for a struggle both men saw to be inevitable, Churchill geared himself for the first time to a task worthy of his strength. This was no momentary flicker of adventurousness, like his Boer War escape or the Sidney Street incident, but a long, weary pull in which former convictions found to be inadequate had to be ruthlessly scrapped and plans, years ahead of their time, pushed through against the killing weight of well-meaning vote-regarding inertia.

The man who, on his own responsibility, mobilised the Fleet in 1914 was obviously a man of stature, one nothing could stop but some colossal misjudgment. Such a misjudgment was provided, in the opinion of some, by the Gallipoli campaign, and Churchill suffered as the scapegoat for a plan which had from its inception been doomed to failure by the lack of enthusiasm for it amongst almost all his responsible colleagues.

Where another man might have retired in high dudgeon to some safe post of unimpeachable respectability, Churchill's only gesture was to thrust himself into the battle as an officer on the Western Front.

His return later to the political scene was marked by an avalanche of political problems, many of which —such as the question of a unified Ireland and a fair Arab-Jewish settlement in the Middle-East—have remained insoluble to this day. Where a solution could be achieved, as in the near-fiasco of the de-mobilisation, he achieved it speedily and to the general satisfaction. Elsewhere his compromises worked, which was about all that could reasonably be hoped. At any rate he proved himself at this time

MOMENT OF DEFIANCE—1940

singularly unafraid of making potentially unpopular decisions and, as he was to point out in similar circumstances at a later period of his life, no one else seemed particularly eager to make them for him.

The years in the political wilderness before the Second World War were the years with Fisher all over again, but now he was fighting alone and from almost outside the official machine. How easy it would have been then to become merely the prophet of woe, the self-satisfied voice ready to say in 1939, " I told you so. "

That was not Churchill's way. His way was to find what most needed to be done and to put drive, charm, and where necessary bluff into getting it done. When the moment came he knew the soldiers to encourage, the scientists to promote; he possessed more accurate information about the enemy than the Government, and from a little-regarded committee of which he had contrived to get himself made a member, had nursed the invention that was to save his country in its first crucial battle—radar.

Yet, when war came, all his hard-earned knowledge was put, without a word of reproach or recrimination, at the disposal of the man whose policy had been so utterly opposed to his own, and when that man's health finally broke under the burden it was Churchill who made the most moving defence of his character, policy and achievements.

As a leader in war Churchill had to win and keep the confidence of the people, of Parliament and of the Service Chiefs. To the first he gave a clear picture of their plight, warm sympathy in their afflictions and a trumpet call to action. To the second he gave the realisation of his unrivalled grasp of the grand design that must unfold through the years ahead. To the last he brought the sure knowledge that they might take calculated risks of even the most hair-raising kind without having to look over their shoulders.

Never content with the passive role, his strategy was always based on attack. Sometimes that attack had to be envisaged as coming far in the future, yet the planning for it was always given first priority in his thoughts and actions. Sometimes it could be produced on a small scale, as in the early commando raids, and here it had at once his active sympathy and practical, heartening support.

There has sometimes been propounded a theory that in modern war forces should be led from behind. Neither Churchill nor his great General, Montgomery, ever found this theory very attractive.

Where the bombing was worst, there Churchill would be, and only the direct intervention of King George VI prevented him from arriving as an interested observer (or, who knows, even a participant in the struggle) on the D-Day beaches.

That was his way, and it was the knowledge of such things that for millions turned Winston into " Winnie ", making them see the " V " sign and the brandished cigar not as tricks but as genuine expressions of a larger-than-life, heroic personality.

At that time Churchill's words were the testament of the Free World. But if Churchill had spoken only *to* its people his words would not have continued to echo with ever-growing resonance down the years; it was his unique gift to speak in their darkest hour *for* the people, and having become their mouthpiece so to remain till sorrow and loss were swallowed up in victory.

In those days his words took on a new force, a new simplicity. He was no longer speaking, in his addresses to the nations, in order to convince them—events had done that; he was making a testament of faith. Those speeches, the most widely diffused the world has ever known, were yet in a sense among the most private. They were those each man would wish to make with his own soul in his personal hour of reckoning: the only soul Churchill addressed was that of the world: " This is the lesson: never give in, never give in, never, never, never—in nothing great or small, large or petty—never give in except to convictions of honour and good sense "; " Neither the sudden shock of battle, nor the long-drawn trials of vigilance and exertion will wear us down "; " This is indeed the grand heroic period of our history, and the light of glory shines on all "; " Whatever happens we shall endure to the end ".

The grating, measured tones are still. Only the historical record remains. The man is dead, yet in the hearts of millions the grateful memory will live of one who, whatever the burden, never faltered as leader, inspiration, exemplar of his age.

ILLUSTRIOUS ANCESTORS

Some families produce eminent men for generation after generation, but genius is usually solitary. Where it comes from no-one knows : it seldom perpetuates itself. The Nelsons, Napoleons and Cromwells blaze up from obscurity and with their deaths the strain carries on as though it had never bred such unlikely creatures. Winston Leonard Spencer Churchill, born on the thirtieth of November, 1874 came of a family that had already played a leading part twice in the nation's story and he has always been, rightly, very conscious of its glories. Many boys look to the future with the vaguest of aspirations, but to Winston the " glories of our blood and state " were from the first both a guiding light and the mark at which one aimed. He was born to the benevolent exercise of power, as practised by his father, and also to the knowledge that a man must be ready to lay down his life for what he holds dear or he will not long retain it. Soldiering was in his blood.

JOHN CHURCHILL, DUKE OF MARLBOROUGH, 1650-1722

The founder of the family's fortunes had been one of the ablest generals in England's history. It was in appreciation for his great victory over the French and Bavarian armies at *Blenheim* that he was given, by Queen Anne and his country, the palace of that name—in which Winston was born. Winston's father, Lord Randolph Churchill, 1849-95 (right) had risen to a position of great power within the Conservative party in the ' eighties ' by his realisation of the need for " Tory democracy ", a socially-conscious policy likely to appeal to the great new electorate then being enfranchised. Later Winston was to write of his father with deep sympathy and understanding. Later, also, he was in his early years as a politician to echo Lord Randolph's pleas for " retrenchment and reform."

LORD RANDOLPH CHURCHILL, 1849–95

WINSTON WITH HIS MOTHER AND HIS YOUNGER BROTHER JOHN
BLENHEIM PALACE

THE SCHOOLBOY

One of the major influences in Winston's life was the fact that mixed with his English blood was another strain deriving from his American mother, Jennie Jerome, daughter of the fabulous millionaire Leonard Jerome. Apart from its general bearing on his character, this connection with the New World was to stand him in good stead when American sympathy and help of the " lease-lend " variety were so urgently needed in the early years of the Second World War. Here Winston is seen (opposite) with his mother and brother, and here too is Blenheim Palace, a symbol of continuity in national affairs not lost on the boy who was later to say, " it is in adversity . . . that the character of our slowly-wrought institutions reveals its latent, invincible strength."

As a schoolboy Winston showed little promise of brilliance. Lord Randolph who had hoped to see him established at the bar was forced to change his mind and let him adopt an army career. At Harrow, however, Winston did give two clear signs of his potentialities by becoming the Public Schools Fencing Champion and by winning a prize for a faultless recitation of a large slice of the *Lays of Ancient Rome*. The picture below shows a view of the Old Schools at Harrow.

HARROW SCHOOL

ARMY CADET

THE YOUNG OFFICER

At Sandhurst the young Churchill was faced for the first time with information that seemed to him worth acquiring, information which could be applied in action. He worked hard and played hard with the result that in 1894 he passed out eighth in a batch of one hundred and fifty—and having acquired that love of horses that was later to enliven his leisure with the delights of polo and racing. The army practice of honouring with real devotion institutions and customs, which are with another part of the mind looked upon as mildly comical or even irrelevant, was very much in the Churchill pattern of preserving the past but altering one's attitude to it in the light of present needs. Later, visits to Harrow, the scene of his inauspicious start in life, were to demonstrate the same mixture of loyalty and humorous insight.

AT THE AGE OF TWENTY-ONE

SUBALTERN IN INDIA

In January 1895 Lord Randolph died. With him died Winston's hopes of aiding him to regain the great place from which he had been ousted. In March Winston joined the *4th Hussars* (above). During the next three years he saw garrison service in England and India but contrived to get a far wider experience of active service conditions than most of his contemporaries. First he took part as an observer in the Cuban War, then later in India he got himself attached to two fighting expeditions. It was about this time also that he laid the foundations of two of his future "careers"—as historian and journalist —with a book *The Malakand Field Force* and with articles for the *Daily Telegraph* designed to pay the cost of his unofficial "attachments". Finally he contrived to take part in Kitchener's Sudan expedition, including the last full-scale cavalry charge at Omdurman.

£25

(Twenty-five Pounds stg.) REWARD is offered by the Sub-Commission of the fifth division, on behalf of the Special Constable of the said division, to anyone who brings the escaped prisioner of war

CHURCHILL,

dead or alive to this office.

For the Sub-Commission of the fifth division,
(Signed) LODK. de HAAS, Sec.

DURBAN – 1899

THE SOUTH AFRICAN WAR

Churchill now determined to go into politics and resigned his commission. In 1899 he stood for one of the two Conservative seats at Old-ham but lost it by fifteen hundred votes. Almost immediately, however, the South African War broke out and he at once set off as the correspondent of the *Morning Post*. While in pursuit of a " scoop ", the armoured train in which he was riding was derailed by the Boers. Churchill—his non-combatant status for-gotten—set about organising its defence but was captured. Treated leniently, under the circumstances, as a prisoner of war, he escaped dramati-cally and in spite of the £25 reward offered for his re-capture made his way to Durban where he was feted as a hero and had to address the crowd.

FIRST STEPS IN POLITICS

As a man in the public eye he found no difficulty in getting elected at Oldham in 1900 and spoke strongly in Parliament on behalf of the defeated Boers. In 1904, following his father's doctrine of "retrenchment" in the Service Estimates and in support of Free Trade, Churchill became a Liberal. Elected for Manchester North West in December 1905, he was soon in Office, first under Sir Henry Campbell Bannerman and later under Herbert Asquith as, successively, Under-Secretary of State for the Colonies, President of the Board of Trade and, in 1910, Home Secretary. By the latter date he had lost his Manchester seat but had gained another in Dundee. These pictures show him in 1908, electioneering in Manchester and at No. 10 Downing Street.

MRS. CHURCHILL

In 1908 Churchill married Miss Clementine Ogilvie Hozier who was to aid him so much throughout his career by her methodical, disciplined yet unobtrusive ordering of his household, and by an inflexible power of " getting things done " second only to his own. At this time too began his interest in social amelioration, fostered by his friendship with David Lloyd George, also a growing realisation of the menace of Germany's armed might.

14

SIDNEY STREET

A hint of the melodramatic streak in Churchill's nature was revealed by the Sidney Street affair (1911). On this occasion a gang of desperate criminals had been cornered in a house in Whitechapel and as Home Secretary he insisted on involving himself in the proceedings. The Home Secretary's place was obviously at his desk, to which would flow in due course official reports on the progress of the siege. To Churchill, however, inaction in the face of danger was unthinkable. Frowned on at the time, this exploit showed a trait later not unwelcome in bomb-scarred London. At the scene of the battle (below); giving evidence at the subsequent enquiry (right).

With one eye now constantly turned to Germany, Churchill made a point of finding his way there in 1913 to watch the German army manoeuvres. He is seen here (above) with the Kaiser and (below) with F. E. Smith later to be Lord Chancellor. At home Churchill was working to integrate the plans of the Army and the Navy for landing a force on the continent should it be necessary. Jellicoe, a comparatively junior officer, had been made Second in Command of the Home Fleet, the Navy had been given new speed by changing over from coal to oil and a new punch by the inclusion of 15 inch guns (a dangerous innovation, many thought) in its latest battleships.

FIRST WORLD WAR

Though preparing for what now seemed to him the certainty of war, Churchill was no warmonger. Here he is seen with Sir Edward Grey who, as Foreign Secretary, worked so hard for peace but who with Churchill, was insistent, when Belgium's neutrality was violated in August 1914, that we must stand by our pledge to defend her.

Throughout his years at the Admiralty Churchill had worked to build up a fleet that would be ready when "the day" came. As the war clouds gathered he had organised a test mobilisation and entirely on his own authority had finally despatched the fleet to its action stations. A week later had come war—and his justification.

This picture shows ships of the First Battle Squadron in line, H.M.S. *Royal Sovereign* (nearest camera), H.M.S. *Resolution* and H.M.S. *Revenge*. The five ships of the *Royal Sovereign* class, mounting eight 15 inch and fourteen 6 inch guns and with a service speed of 22 knots, were the last battleships to be built for the British Fleet during the First World War.

17

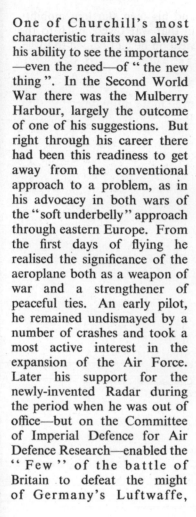

One of Churchill's most characteristic traits was always his ability to see the importance —even the need—of " the new thing ". In the Second World War there was the Mulberry Harbour, largely the outcome of one of his suggestions. But right through his career there had been this readiness to get away from the conventional approach to a problem, as in his advocacy in both wars of the "soft underbelly" approach through eastern Europe. From the first days of flying he realised the significance of the aeroplane both as a weapon of war and a strengthener of peaceful ties. An early pilot, he remained undismayed by a number of crashes and took a most active interest in the expansion of the Air Force. Later his support for the newly-invented Radar during the period when he was out of office—but on the Committee of Imperial Defence for Air Defence Research—enabled the " Few " of the battle of Britain to defeat the might of Germany's Luftwaffe,

TOP, VISITING THE CENTRAL FLYING SCHOOL, SEPTEMBER, 1912

CENTRE, A FLIGHT OVER PORTSMOUTH HARBOUR, 1914

BOTTOM, ON A TRANSATLANTIC FLIGHT TO THE BERMUDA CONFERENCE, 1942

WEAPONS

and his own startling mobility in that war owed much to the weapon he had helped to forge. Yet with the tank, the other great factor in the modern "war of mobility" he had an even more intimate connection. It was during his tenure of the Admiralty in the First World War that his mind turned to the problem of how to circumvent the stalemate of trench warfare on the Western Front. There, defence, based on the machine-gun, the mortar and heavy artillery, rendered attack hideously wasteful and almost useless.—But if something immune to bullets and capable of straddling trenches could be evolved?—From this germ came the "landships", experimented with during his Admiralty days. And from the landship came the tank that, largely wasted in the First World War, later came into its own in the Western Desert at the grave risk—deliberately undertaken by Churchill—of leaving England almost defenceless against possible invasion.

TOP, EARLY TANK TRIALS IN 1916

CENTRE, TANKS IN SERVICE ON THE WESTERN FRONT, 1917

BOTTOM, THE PRIME MINISTER INSPECTING A CROMWELL TANK, 1944

GALLIPOLI

Gallipoli, name evocative of such heroism and such appalling losses, was the scene of an attempt to neutralise Turkey and link up with Russia by a great diversionary thrust at the enemy's back door. The plan for a naval action to force the Dardanelles was called off by the admiral on the spot after heavy but not crippling losses ; the land forces were not made available in time : the coast was heavily fortified under German supervision during the period of delay, and the final landings could not be successfully maintained.

Removed from the Admiralty, because of his supposed responsibility for the Dardanelles fiasco, Churchill was given the "consolation prize" of Chancellor of the Duchy of Lancaster. But this post with its non-existent duties was not one to appeal to such a man in danger's hour, and 1916 found him on the Western Front, commanding the *6th Royal Scots Fusiliers*, as usual dressed somewhat unconventionally for the part. At first Churchill's arrival was hailed as anything but a blessing by his superior officers. Well acquainted with the spectacular figure he had cut in the past as politician, reporter and naval strategist, they did not realise the capacity for taking pains, the burning enthusiasm, the fearlessness and the genuine gift for leadership upon which the "spectacular figure" was based. They were soon convinced. Those he led needed no convincing.

WITH THE PRINCE OF WALES, 1919

Having organised an immense output of munitions for 1919, Churchill found himself put out of a job by the German collapse in 1918. But he had now acquired a reputation as a " trouble-shooter " and Lloyd George made him Secretary of State for War and Air (1918-1921). Here he is seen with the Prince of Wales whom, as King Edward VIII, he was to stand by so tenaciously at the time of the abdication crisis.

POLITICS IN THE 1920's

The years immediately following the war were to confront Churchill with many problems; all of them demanding immediate solution, many of them, in fact, insoluble. First came the question of demobilisation, which Churchill answered with a scheme of 'first in, first out' which took into account both the soldier's age and the number of times he had been wounded. The problems of withdrawing from Archangel the force committed to defending the White Russians against the new regime, of making a settlement between Jews and Arabs in Palestine and of settling the explosive issue of Ireland's independence were all matters he had to handle either as Secretary for War and Air or as Secretary for the Colonies (1921-

1922). Later, when the declining Liberal power appeared to be throwing in its weight with the new force of Labour, Churchill stood as an Independent for the Abbey Division of Westminster where he was defeated by a narrow margin. In November 1924 the Conservative Party, ready to support anyone who would oppose the Labour Party after its year of power, allowed Churchill to contest the Epping Division of Essex, unopposed by them, as a Constitutionalist and he was duly elected. From 1924 to 1929 he held the office of Chancellor of the Exchequer, a period which saw the return of the country to the gold standard, and the General Strike.

ELECTIONEERING IN THE ABBEY DIVISION OF WESTMINSTER IN 1924

SPORTS AND PASTIMES

A man of wide interests and bursting with activity, Churchill obviously believed in the old adage that " all work and no play makes Jack a dull boy ". Any *less* " dull boy " it would be hard to find. Yet he was by no means the " Jack of all trades " who is " master of none ". As orator, historian and journalist he had few rivals to fear; as a painter he commanded the respect of the knowledgeable. As Parliamentarian and Statesman he was of course unique—and even as bricklayer the edifices he constructed were acknowledged to be sound. But above all he was a whole man— never content to exalt the mind at the expense of the body or to let a skilful brain rob him of a skilful hand. Contemplation was never his strong suit (though when reverses forced him to it, it bore notable fruit), nor had the pursuit of knowledge for its own sake ever attracted him. But what the brain or the hand can be set to *do*, what the brain or the hand can be made visibly to *bring about*, that— especially, if it involved some element of risk—he would undertake. Fishing or shooting he looked constricted; with a golf club he looked miserable: it is almost impossible to imagine him with a billiard cue. But given a medium of expression allowing for the sweeping gesture, for dash and bravura, he was at home—and usually " in the forefront of the battle ".

RIGHT, PHEASANT SHOOTING IN 1910

BELOW, BUILDING A HOUSE AT WESTERHAM, KENT IN 1928, HELPED BY HIS DAUGHTER, SARAH

HUNTING THE WILD BOAR IN FRANCE, 1927

ON A PAINTING HOLIDAY IN MADEIRA, 1950

INTO THE POLITICAL WILDERNESS

The world of figures in which a Chancellor of the Exchequer dwells allows of little "showmanship", provides few excitements and few tangible enemies to be overwhelmed by craft or force—it is not a Churchillian world. Nor was Stanley Baldwin a Churchillian Prime Minister. There were of course good wordy duels with Snowdon in the Commons, and the annual ritual of the budget with its enigmatic smiles and case full of secrets, yet probably it was with some relief that Churchill found himself electioneering again in 1929. But now it seemed that the tide turned against him. Ramsay MacDonald returned to power, and a nation tired of war began to dream that because the world longed for peace it had found it.

Churchill had no such illusions. In 1932 he was already pointing to "the great mass of Russia, with its enormous armies" and warning the country, "If you wish for disarmament, it will be necessary to go to the political and economic causes which lie behind the maintenance of armies and navies". At the same time he spoke most emphatically against acceptance of the concept of "total war" and the bombing of open cities.

CHURCHILL, ACCOMPANIED BY HIS DAUGHTER DIANA, ON HIS WAY TO THE HOUSE OF COMMONS IN 1928 TO PRESENT HIS LAST BUDGET

ON BOARD H.M.S. "ENCHANTRESS" AT
THE FLEET REVIEW, 1937

In the long years "in the wilderness"
three of Churchill's qualities showed up
in all their brightness—his foresight,
his perseverance and his loyalty. He
warned his country and kept on warning
it in the face of apathy, anger and
ridicule. He served his king and
continued serving him to the last
moment without thought of the effect
on his own position or career.

Of course the wilderness had its own
consolations ; family life with Mrs.
Churchill—seen here in a characteristi-
cally cheerful pose—and with his
children ; time to paint, time to write
—we must thank it for *Marlborough*,
the four volume life of his great ancestor.
Yet, in spite of the cheerfulness, in spite
of the hint of "Admiralty" in this
picture taken in 1937 aboard H.M.S.
Enchantress, Churchill was really waiting
for the call that came in 1939.

MRS. CHURCHILL AT A TENNIS PARTY

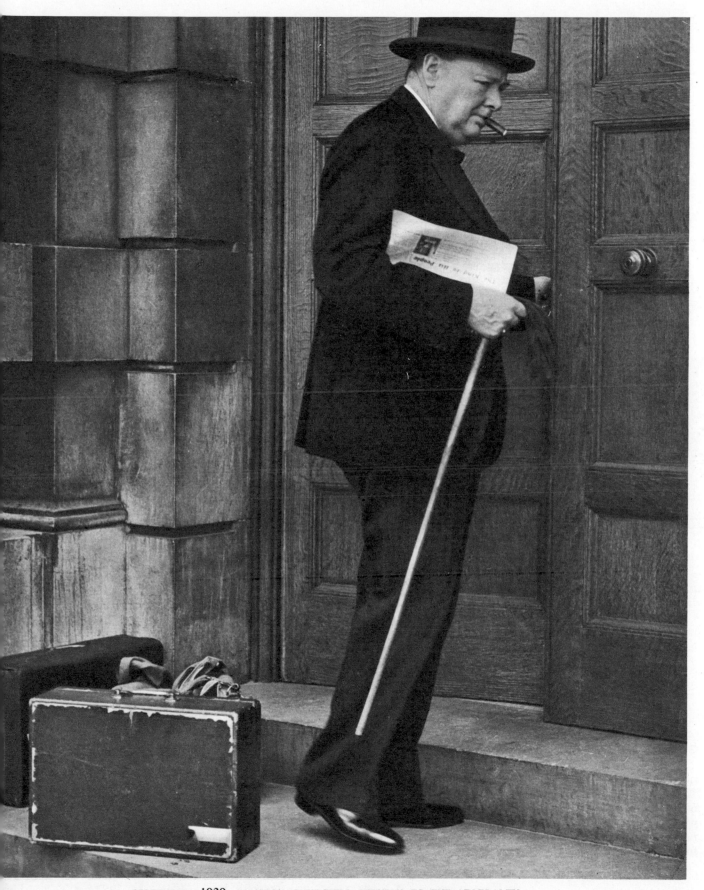

SEPTEMBER, 1939, WINSTON CHURCHILL RETURNS TO THE ADMIRALTY

WAR

Manchuria, Abyssinia, the Rhineland, Axis intervention in Spain, Austria, the Sudetenland, Munich and " peace with honour ", Czechoslovakia ;—the writing had long been on the wall but few had interpreted its fatal message. Now war had come to dismembered Europe and once more, on September 4th, 1939, Churchill was entering the Admiralty as its First Lord.

There was much to be done to safeguard England's seaways. These are the men who—under Churchill's command—saw that it was done—the Board of Admiralty. (Directly under the lamp sits the First Sea Lord and Chief of the Naval Staff, Admiral of the Fleet Sir Dudley Pound.) The arrival of the convoys ; the destruction of the *Graf Spee* in the River Plate ;

the *Cossack's* rescue of the *Altmark* prisoners in a Norwegian fiord—all these speak for the quality of their work. The British expeditionary force too was carried safely to France. Even in these early days of the war it was obvious that Churchill alone amongst the members of Mr. Chamberlain's Cabinet had both the temperament and the knowledge to play " the war game " on the scale and with the temerity that it demanded. In 1938 he had said, " For five years I have talked to the House on these matters—not with very great success. I have watched this famous island descending incontinently, fecklessly, the stairway which leads to a dark gulf." Yet brought back from the wilderness in the hour of need he bore no grudge and was the first to pay tribute to the principles of the leader whose " appeasement " policy he had fought so relentlessly.

THE BOARD OF ADMIRALTY IN SESSION

THE FIRST YEAR OF WAR

In a country woefully unprepared there was much to do, but mercifully there was a lull before the storm, in the shape of the nine month " phoney war ". In this time Churchill " looked to his moat " both at the Admiralty, and on personal visits to England's many miles of coastal defences. He might have said then, as he was to say later, " we have our faults, and our social system has its faults, but we hope that, with God's help, we shall be able to prove for all time, or at any rate, for a long time, that a State or Commonwealth of democracy, possesses amid the sharpest shocks the faculty of survival in a high and honourable and, indeed, in a glorious degree."

February 1940. Here is the Churchill that the world was to come to know so well. Under the guns of the *Exeter* (overleaf) he speaks to her crew on their return from the River Plate. The " greyhounds " had been loosed from the " slips " and they had done their work well. He surveys them with a sombre, a humble, a determined pride and stands rock-like before them to render thanks.

INSPECTING DEFENCES OF SOUTHERN COMMAND, 1940

ADDRESSING THE CREW OF H.M.S. " EXETER " ON THEIR RETURN FROM THE SINKING OF THE " GRAF SPEE "
AT THE BATTLE OF THE RIVER PLATE

MR. CHURCHILL'S WAR CABINET IN THE SPRING OF 1941

Mr. Churchill's War Cabinet (as in the Spring of 1941), (back row: left to right) Mr. Arthur Greenwood, *Minister without Portfolio*; Mr. Ernest Bevin, *Minister of Labour*; Lord Beaverbrook, *Minister of Aircraft Production*; Sir Kingsley Wood, *Chancellor of the Exchequer*. (Front row: left to right) Sir John Anderson, *Lord President of the Council*; Mr. Winston Churchill, *Prime Minister*; Mr. Clement Attlee, *Lord Privy Seal*; Mr. Anthony Eden, *Foreign Secretary*.

OUR FINEST HOUR

Now England stood alone in her " finest hour ". With an army half of whose arms and equipment had had to be left on the beaches of France she awaited invasion, and with a handful of fighter planes, Spitfires (below) and Hurricanes, she challenged—and by the end of September had broken—the power of Germany's Luftwaffe. " Never in the field of human conflict was so much owed by so many to so few." For the rest it was " blood, toil, tears and sweat " that Churchill offered. New forces and weapons had to be prepared, but in the meantime the Churchill spirit fired the country through his broadcasts, and the Commandos —an institution after his own heart—offered a foretaste of better things to the people of subjugated Europe.

Meanwhile London was " taking it ". Never had a city withstood such a prolonged and terrible ordeal. Above St. Paul's the vapour trails turned and twisted (opposite), and by night the sky glowed redly behind the great dome and the Cross. The Anderson shelter became a feature of most back gardens ; the late traveller in the Underground saw ranks of sleepers swathed in overcoats and rugs lining the platforms ; firewatchers paced the rooftops and Wardens herded their often reluctant charges out of sight, if not out of hearing, of the battle. And undismayed Churchill was saying, " even if all the homes of the country be levelled, then we shall still be found standing together to build them up again after the fighting is over."

FIGHTERS OVER ST. PAUL'S

33

FIRES ROUND ST. PAUL'S

HURRICANES

THE SINKING OF THE " BISMARCK "

THE TURNING POINT, 1941

1941 was the turning point of the war. Britain entered it alone, financially at a low ebb, menaced with starvation by her shipping losses in the Atlantic, successful admittedly in North Africa but only against the weaker of the Axis partners, Italy. But the weapons were being made—Churchill was there to try them; the convoys, with increasingly active assistance from America were getting through—Churchill was there to thank and encourage their crews. Yet there were many disasters to be faced. Greece was supported in her struggle and lost. Crete was lost. In North Africa Rommel pushed back our army, depleted by these campaigns, to the borders of Egypt. Yet Churchill's attitude remained what it had been in 1940 to his commanders in the field;—they must be trusted and supported. " I have endeavoured always to say that those who launch themselves against the enemy in any action, with vigour and violence will, whatever the upshot, receive the support of His Majesty's Government." In Parliament there was strong criticism of the government, especially after the sinking of the *Hood*, a graceful but old and all too vulnerable battle-cruiser in which armour had been sacrificed to speed. Churchill rode the flood, not as a dictator—though he could be dictatorial—but in the clear knowledge that he remained the man for the job. In his humility, however, there was always likely to be steel. " I do not at all resent criticism, even when, for the sake of emphasis, it for a time parts company with reality."—The *Bismarck* was sunk (above): the *Hood* was avenged.

35

MAY, 1941

Mr. Churchill contemplates the ruins of the House of Commons, bombed in May 1941. " We must have spirits so constant that we can derive from misfortune added strength. . . . We cannot tell how long the road will be. We only know that it will be stony, painful and uphill, and that we shall march along it to the end."

PRESIDENT ROOSEVELT MEETS THE PRIME MINISTER, 1941

THE PRIME MINISTER AND THE PRESIDENT ON BOARD U.S.S. "AUGUSTA"

" BUT WESTWARD, LOOK, THE LAND IS BRIGHT "

As 1941 passed by, Churchill could fairly quote Clough's line " but westward, look, the land is bright." Under President Roosevelt, the United States was gradually becoming more and more openly implicated in the struggle. " Lease lend " had brought England much needed escort vessels. Wendell Wilkie had come to England as Roosevelt's personal representative to meet Churchill. Finally Premier and President had met in the middle of the Atlantic, aboard the U.S. Cruiser *Augusta*, and had drawn up a joint statement of faith for the future—*The Atlantic Charter*. This union, already so strong, was to be cemented in the last month of the year by disaster. America was to suffer at Pearl Harbour her most crippling naval loss of all time with the undeclared entry of Japan into the war, and Britain was to see her Far Eastern Empire begin to crumble under the assault of the same enemy after the loss of the *Repulse* and the *Prince of Wales*. —Yet at last America was in the war and that fact outweighed all others. Churchill did not leave the Americans to imagine the welcome he owed them but posted off again across the Atlantic to address the Senate. " Now that we are together, now that we are linked in a righteous comradeship of arms . . . a new scene opens upon which a steady light will glow and brighten."

JANUARY, 1942, MR. CHURCHILL ADDRESSING A JOINT SESSION OF THE U.S. CONGRESS

THE WESTERN DESERT

The pictures on this page show Churchill on a visit to the Eighth Army in the Western desert during August, 1942. (Right) with General Freyberg, Commander of the 2nd New Zealand Division and (below) with General Wavell who had borne the brunt as Commander in this theatre during the early years but had been succeeded by General Auchinleck, who was now to give way to General Alexander. 1942 had begun disastrously with the loss of Malaya and Singapore to the Japanese and in the desert things had gone little better. But now with General Montgomery in command of the Eighth Army the tide turned. His great victory against Rommel at El Alamein was the result, partly of his own brilliance, partly of the planned build-up of supplies pushed ahead with by Churchill during the dark days of 1941. From now on Montgomery was to drive Rommel westwards until, with the aid of the Americans, Africa was eventually cleared of Axis troops by May 1943. From there the first attack was to be launched on Europe as General Alexander swept through Sicily in July 1943 and on to Italy in September. Meanwhile Russia after a " scorched earth " retreat to Stalingrad had stopped the German advance and was taking terrible toll of the invader——

WITH GENERAL FREYBERG

IN CAIRO WITH GENERAL SIR ARCHIBALD WAVELL AND LT.-COL. SIR SIKANDER HYAT KHAN

SHAKING HANDS WITH A SERGEANT OF AN ARMOURED BRIGADE

INSPECTING COMMANDOS

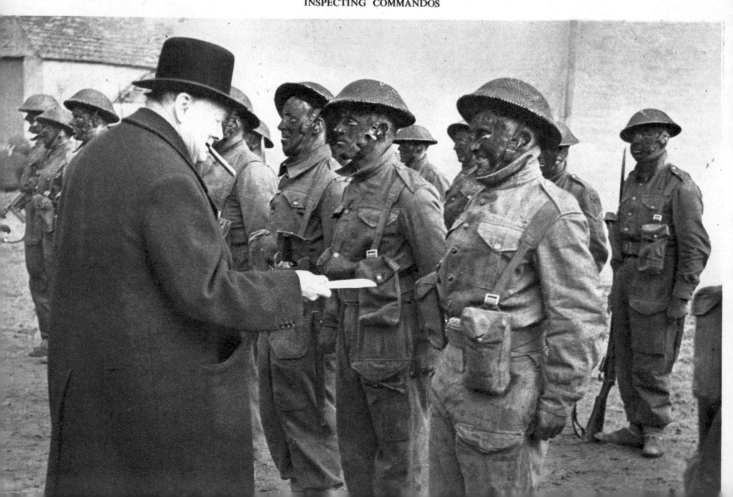

PLANNING FOR VICTORY

——But back in England all thoughts were directed to the "Second Front" for which Russia was clamouring and which now began to seem, for the first time, a practical possibility. Behind all the preparations were the drive and energy of the Prime Minister as he bombarded the service ministries with memoranda, worked through a ceaseless round of visits to units (such as the commandos opposite) pressed the necessary measures through Parliament and by his broadcasts carried the nation forward from the spirit of " we can take it " to the idea of " the liberation of Europe ". In operation " Overlord " the *21st Army Group* under General Montgomery was to take the lead, but even this immense undertaking was for Churchill only one facet of a world-wide situation for which he had to plan: The links with a Russia who demanded much—and was prepared to give little—in co-operation, had to be cemented by a further meeting at Teheran between Roosevelt, Stalin and Churchill. Plans had to be laid for the re-conquest of the Far East in co-operation with the U.S.A. and China.

1943, STALIN, ROOSEVELT AND CHURCHILL AT THE TEHERAN CONFERENCE

AMBULANCES USING A MULBERRY PIER

MULBERRY

When the invasion of Europe came on June 6th, 1944 it turned out to be quite unlike any operation staged before. In the past any landing made in strength against an enemy coast had always necessitated the capture of a port. Even with the amazing advances made by the Americans in the use of amphibious landing craft for getting men, vehicles and tanks ashore, no adequate build-up of supplies could have been maintained without a port had it not been for the *Mulberries*. In these movable harbours, large towable units could be fixed in place off the coast to act as floating piers, rising and falling with the tide. Protected by old merchant ships and caissons sunk further out to form a breakwater and connected to the shore by pontoon bridges (as shown here), they were capable of handling very heavy traffic. For this invention, which left the allied commanders free to choose their landing place where it would cause the most surprise and meet the least opposition, we have, at least in part, to thank Mr. Churchill— for the idea evolved from a memorandum of his, produced several years earlier.

The rest of the plans for the invasion had been made with the same mixture of boldness, ingenuity and attention to detail. Reconnaissance raids, and a mass of holiday snapshots of the French coast, collected from the British public as the result of an appeal, had given an idea of the problem to be faced. Frogmen were trained for dealing with under-water obstacles. A process was evolved for "waterproofing" vehicles so that they could wade ashore. "*Pluto*" the pipeline that was to carry petrol under the Channel had been constructed.

THE INVASION

On *D. Day* General Eisenhower, Supreme Commander Allied Powers in Europe had said in his order of the day, " The eyes of the world are upon you. The hopes and prayers of liberty-loving people everywhere march with you." No-one could have been more eager to carry his prayers with the invading army in person than Churchill, but his plea was understandably and wisely over-ruled. Yet only six days later he crosses the Channel and soon after is getting his first view of the new battlefields and talking in Caen to troops who took part in the initial assault. After a pause to consolidate, the allied armies are off across Europe towards a Germany that through the years has lost command of the air and has been bombed to the point where her industries are failing her——

——But Hitler has still two unpleasant surprises in reserve for England,—surprises that owing to the same cause have had to wait overlong to be effective. The flying bomb and the rocket are loosed on London to do their wanton damage, but as the allied forces sweep northwards and their launching sites are captured the menace is overcome.

MR. CHURCHILL, WITH ADMIRAL VIAN AND F.M. SIR ALAN BROOKE, ON HIS WAY TO THE NORMANDY BEACHES

WITH THE TROOPS IN NORMANDY

A FLYING BOMB TAKES OFF   A V.I. INCIDENT, JULY, 1944

MR. CHURCHILL WITH THE COMMONWEALTH PRIME MINISTERS

For all Churchill's foreign contacts in matters of strategy and post-war planning, it is never absent from his mind that he is working not only for a country and for an alliance of friendly nations but also for the linked British Commonwealth and Empire. Here he is seen in more peaceful surroundings at a conference of Commonwealth Premiers held shortly before D. Day. With him are (left to right) General Smuts, *South Africa*; Mr. Mackenzie King, *Canada*; Mr. J. Curtin, *Australia*; and Mr. Peter Fraser, *New Zealand*.

Peace in Europe is now in sight. The invading armies are over the Rhine, after the Germans' last desperate throw, the Ardennes offensive. Churchill is there to see, to cross the Rhine also and to talk with Eisenhower the Commander with whom his relations have always been so friendly and so successful. But for long months now Churchill's main preoccupation has been the world that must be rebuilt after the war. There is still Japan to be dealt with but, once the allies can concentrate their full strength against her, victory is only a matter of time. But what will Russia do ? Perhaps he regrets that cherished plan of his—the invasion through Eastern Europe. Now Russia has swallowed Eastern Europe. Roosevelt trusts her ; Churchill does not. For some time it has been evident that Stalin has been working on that fear of " British Imperialism ", native to every American, in his dealings with Roosevelt. For Churchill, a thorough European as well as a world statesman, the old idea of the " Balance of Power " still seems to be vital unless and until something better can be worked out. For many hundreds of years England has believed that no continental power must be allowed to grow to a strength that will endanger its neighbours. The policy has not always worked but it appears that—as the dentist says—" things would have been much worse without it."

45

WITH THE SUPREME COMMANDER, GENERAL EISENHOWER

ACROSS THE RHINE

KING GEORGE VI WITH HIS WAR CABINET, INCLUDING MR. CHURCHILL, MR. ATTLEE AND MR. BEVIN

V.E. DAY AT BUCKINGHAM PALACE

MR. CHURCHILL'S V.E. DAY BROADCAST

BRITISH VICTORY PARADE IN BERLIN, JULY, 1945

MR. CHURCHILL, GENERALISSIMO STALIN, AND PRESIDENT TRUMAN MEET IN BERLIN, JULY, 1945

Mr. Churchill went to Berlin for the Victory Parade in July 1945. 10,000 men representing Britain's Fighting Services marched past him in the Charlottenburger Chaussee for 40 minutes. Mr. Churchill inspected the tanks of the *Desert Rats* in company with Field Marshal Sir Bernard Montgomery and Field Marshal Sir Alan Brooke. Two days later the three Chiefs of State meet. Roosevelt, that generous, courageous, perhaps over-optimistic man, is dead and has been succeeded by President Truman. The atmosphere seems cordial. But half way around the world the " cloud no bigger than a man's hand " is waiting to " mushroom " over Hiroshima and Nagasaki. That, more than the friendly smiles, is what now preserves peace between the western and eastern allies.

1947, MR. CHURCHILL, AS HONORARY AIR COMMODORE OF 615 SQUADRON, R.A.F., REVISITS BIGGIN HILL

THE FAMOUS V-SIGN

Victory at the polls in 1951 and Mr. Churchill is once again Prime Minister. " V for Victory " implies
no " devil take the hindmost " reversal of what has been good in the Welfare State but a policy of
expansion at home and " containment " abroad.

RELAXATION

In the intervals of working for a closer relationship between France and Germany and smoothing out the rough places of Anglo-American co-operation; between efforts to come to grips with the Russian problem by arranging top-level talks; between troubles about the Canal Zone, troubles soon to arise in Malaya and Kenya and the ever-present knowledge of war raging in Korea, the Prime Minister could enjoy few moments of real relaxation. Chartwell Manor, his home in Kent, was the scene of most of them.

The background to his thoughts and labours while in the political wilderness so many years ago, Chartwell was waiting to receive him into its peace when his mighty labours for his country's, and the world's, safety were done. This was Churchill's home, when he was not officially in residence at No. 10 Downing Street. Here he wrote many of his books, composed many of his speeches, entertained, relaxed, " made improvements " (notably with bricks and mortar) and gathered his family around him.

CHARTWELL MANOR

MR. AND MRS. CHURCHILL AT CHARTWELL ON MR. CHURCHILL'S 77TH BIRTHDAY

THE CHURCHILL FAMILY

Seeing politicians always on the hustings or against the background of " the best club in the world "—as the Mother of Parliaments has been called—it is easy to forget that each of them has behind his public self his own private life, his *home* life. Father of a son and four daughters (one of whom died in infancy),

Mr. Churchill has been followed in his parliamentary career not only by his son, Randolph, but by his son-in-law, Captain Christopher Soames (married to Mary). His daughter, Sarah, now Lady Audley, is of course the well-known actress, while a niece, Clarissa, is married to Sir Anthony Eden.

SARAH CHURCHILL, THE ACTRESS

MRS. SOAMES, NÉE MARY CHURCHILL

WINSTON CHURCHILL AND HIS GRANDCHILDREN, 1951

AT THE CHRISTENING OF CHARLOTTE SOAMES, NOVEMBER, 1954

MR. CHURCHILL WITH HIS GRANDSON, NICHOLAS SOAMES, IN 1952

On this page two great men are seen in a relaxed mood. Mr. Churchill at the christening of Jeremy Soames, in August, 1952, walks hand in hand with his four-year-old grandson, Nicholas Soames, followed by Field Marshal Viscount Montgomery of Alamein, the new baby's godfather.

KNIGHT COMPANION OF THE GARTER

SIR WINSTON CHURCHILL LEAVING ST. GEORGE'S CHAPEL, WINDSOR AFTER HIS INSTALLATION

On April 24th, 1953 the Queen confers upon the Right Hon. Winston Churchill, M.P. the honour of Knighthood and invests him with the Insignia of a Knight Companion of the Most Noble Order of the Garter. Later, on June 14th, 1954 Sir Winston Churchill is formally installed into the Order in a ceremony at St. George's Chapel, Windsor. During 1953, in Russia, Premier Stalin died, and for a time it seemed possible that under his successor, Mr. Malenkov, an era of greater co-operation might begin. However, with Malenkov's fall next year, the old uncertainties returned, and yet remain.

SIR WINSTON AND LADY CHURCHILL ON THEIR WAY TO WESTMINSTER ABBEY

In May and June of 1953 two great events—happy auguries for England's future—took place within a few days of each other. Sir John Hunt's expedition conquered Everest and England's young and gracious Queen was Crowned at Westminster Abbey. This latter ceremony impressed the world to a totally unexpected degree, not so much by its magnificence as by the quiet dignity and obvious self-dedication of its central figure.

THE PRESENTATION CEREMONY IN WESTMINSTER HALL, NOVEMBER 30, 1954

To mark Sir Winston's eightieth birthday the Lords and the Commons combined to present him with a portrait painted by Mr. Graham Sutherland. Opinions regarding the presentation portrait varied from the lyrical to the vituperative. The Prime Minister's own ambiguous comment, "a remarkable example of modern art" left the scales swinging uneasily.

SIR WINSTON AND LADY CHURCHILL WELCOME THE QUEEN AT NO. 10 DOWNING STREET

Old comrades meet again, in September 1959, in London, at a dinner given by President Eisenhower. With the President and Sir Winston is Field Marshal Lord Alexander.

Sir Winston celebrated his 83rd birthday, November 1957, in the company of Lady Churchill, Lord Montgomery, and his son, Randolph Churchill and his grandson, Randolph's son, Winston.

On 9th April 1963 America signified the depth of her regard for Sir Winston Churchill by granting him honorary citizenship of the United States, an honour never before granted to the subject of another country. Sir Winston was represented in Washington by his son Randolph Churchill, seen above with President John F. Kennedy, and this document and his new U.S.A. passport were presented to him in London by the American Ambassador.

The President of the United States of America

A PROCLAMATION

Whereas

Sir Winston Churchill

a son of America though a subject of Britain, has been throughout his life a firm and steadfast friend of the American people and the American nation; and

Whereas he has freely offered his hand and his faith in days of adversity as well as triumph; and

Whereas his bravery, charity and valor, both in war and in peace, have been a flame of inspiration in freedom's darkest hour; and

Whereas his life has shown that no adversary can overcome, and no fear can deter, free men in the defense of their freedom; and

Whereas he has expressed with unsurpassed power and splendor the aspirations of peoples everywhere for dignity and freedom; and

Whereas he has by his art as an historian and his judgment as a statesman made the past the servant of the future;

Now, Therefore, I, John F. Kennedy, President of the United States of America, under the authority contained in an Act of the 88th Congress, do hereby declare Sir Winston Churchill an honorary citizen of the United States of America.

In Witness Whereof, I have hereunto set my hand and caused the Seal of the United States of America to be affixed.

Done at the City of Washington this ninth day of April in the year of our Lord nineteen hundred and sixty-three, and of the Independence of the United States of America the one hundred and eighty-seventh.

By the President

Acting Secretary of State